KIT

KIT

Megan Barker

CHEERIO

First published in Great Britain in 2023 by Cheerio Publishing

www.cheeriopublishing.com
info@cheeriopublishing.com

10 9 8 7 6 5 4 3 2 1

Typeset in Perpetua by Libanus Press Ltd
Printed and bound in Great Britain by Clays Ltd, Elcograf S.p.A.

ISBN: 978 1 80081 645 9
eISBN: 978 1 80081 892 9

KIT

I OWE YOU A BOOK

Will you write with me?
Shall we hold hands?
I know I am only high noon like this for a limited time.
We can jump together.
One two thr—

SBIGGARNUSALL

Mainly on the street
in the swerve from the campus to the shops
or along the Anniesland canal,
we meet.

Loiter times.
The wander lines.
In and out the West End,
scoring graphite grooves
in the A to Zs we're unfolding in our heads
of this most marcasite city.

You are all trousers.
Clung to the bones where your hips could be?
Fists and fingers seek out the pockets,
lower than your arms can reach
so that your shoulders roll forwards
hang in their sockets –

9

an attitude of someone ready to dig in their heels,
else spring from the hamstrings, take flight.

Often our steps fall in – Hey
journeys converge before – See ya
peeling away.
The flow's unstoppered, we're in the swim, we just take
each other on and take each other off like it's nothing,
like there's plenty of slipway, and anyway, there's that
distance – comes from being 'unavailable' – the
'you'vegotagirlfriendI'vegotaboyfriend' script is in place.
We're not compromising skin, we're just swapping jackets.
(I've still got it. It's hanging in my hall.)

We talk about IT ALL.
The scape is dense with reference –
Lanarkic links –
that A through Z a co-created fabric of connections –
the messh of existence.
With so much time in our hands
to sift and loop and spool our world
we are in each day, in each hour of each day entangled.

The urge, the impulse to create, to frame,
to somehow contain is VIVID.
To make ourselves part of this new-found texture –
This rich humous of political litter!
This cultural material!!
This fermenting firmament of desire!!!
GLASGOW:
grinding, glittering, oil-black machine,
juddering, shuddering, sputuming up petroleum
rainbow sputum that collects in myriad potholes
and soaks our trailing hems like wicks.
We strut about as lamplighters,
inventing it all
God's gifts.
Every wall an opportunity to climb.
It's all we can do not to spurt up all over everything,
spray ourselves silly on every surface, make our mark.
Sublime intervention.

Lowering ourselves down on rope lengths
to an abandoned part of the subway system.
Breathless leaning into the cool wet greening
of the tunnel's halitosis,

the network rumbles and reverberates through us,
and above our heads there are trees, botanics.

Inch by inch –

Darker.

Danker.

Down.

A lone hazel grows up from between the tracks.
A forgotten station.

The concrete walls make of sound
something like silver foil on a filling (is it feedback?).

Somebody's living down there.
There's a sleeping bag and a carrier full of bottles

...Hey man...?

But it's only a recently inhabited shape.
The absence brings us sharply to our presence –

We are ginger on our feet
Fear needles
Have disturbed an ecology

Stirred the must of stagnant indifference
Reawakened a silt of tired sounds.

But as we slide deeper into the darkness, our purpose
dwindles down to the puny nib of the pen in your hand.
After all, what's to be said?
When your blood's full thrumming
but all you have is A–Z.

Engines flooded we light a match.
Out the gloom of our deflation
the tunnel clears its throat,
sputters gutteral utterances in its native tongue.
Speaks:

  Mcnolty got ripped
          JK fukt U first
                  SPAZZA ROOLS
                  I heart Hearts til the DAY I DIY
                        CUNTY
        God Kills
                              Salad Dayz
              Alan takes it hard
  Maggie Winter's mingesbiggarnUSALL

And in the noise and scrawl and dash of hoped-for lives
deeply lived, in the end we just write the date.
Small.   12.11.1998.

You climb the rope last.
Pupils dilating backwards – what's this called?
Pouring dark?
As I ascend, dark **pours** over you.
I see you looking up at me – that squint –
querying the light,
as it touches / empties my head.

Up the flagpole that night,
with battery-powered beats, we come into our bodies.
Pound our AsandZs to GLITTER
Dance the sky an inkblot
Toss woooops at the moon
Try with all our might to lose our ragged
voices to the wind.

LISTS

In bleak weather, over a curry in Bermondsey, you told
me the following:

The City Bee Collective was not all it's cracked up to be

You were lonely doing your PhD

The Academy is a hostile space

The Art World is funded by guns

The obsession in our Culture with the individual artist/
philosopher as Hero leaves no room for community, careful
thinking, meaningful writing, true dialogue or exchange

You organised an electronic jazz night, but only white
men showed up, which was weird

That your upstairs neighbour coveted your garden

The housing cooperative of which you were a part
were uncooperative

But squat life had become unliveable

That you'd got tired of the struggle in this city

But once you know that grass is just green concrete,
it's hard to know where to turn

Some facts you can't unlearn

You only understood how you loved your girlfriend
after she left

Your brother hurts, but he gets by

All the fun has gone out of being a janitor

You had idealised the notion of making a living

And forgot to live

That you had wanted the baby

But you had aborted it all

That these are impossibly infertile conditions

It's crazy, you said, but it's true.

Anyway, enough about me.

How are you? Mac? The twins? And Flo?

I told you the following:

The twins are only interested in their father, who would
rather live free in a ditch, in the olden times way

My daughter never sleeps

My marriage is on its knees

I speak in ultimatums

I have become a gaoler of wild things

I desperately want to feel less desperate

All deep thought has been replaced with lists

I love everyone huge everyone
From a tiny little turret
I built with a pair of loppers

I offered this by way of consolation.
All of this is true today, I said, but tomorrow and
yesterday it may not be.
My thoughts used to run from one day /
line into the next.

I said I had my head in the ground.
You said you thought that maybe for things to begin
again better, we need to welcome disaster in,
let it all fall.

I thought (but didn't say, though you knew I was
thinking it), you are only able to say that because you
have nothing to lose.

You thought (but didn't say, though I knew you were
thinking it, in answer to my unspoken thought),
that is a fundamentally conservative position.
I thought (but didn't say, and I'm not sure if you knew I

was thinking it, though I am sure you yourself were
thinking it but maybe not saying it, even to yourself),
yes but you are lonely and I am not.

As lonely as you.

This was the essence of our conversation: given the
conditions, is it possible not to be lonely?

And we would have held hands if that were the kind of
thing we'd do.

You left most of your balti behind (you who can demolish
anything) and we shambled off to an art show in a
basement somewhere with free cans of Red Stripe on
the door. Inside the gallery a person with a penis sat in
a sterile greenhouse, showed us their G-string, spilled
soiled guts into the body of an acoustic guitar. You didn't
seem to know anyone. You were motionless in the
wash of performed pain. I tried to draw a commentary
from you as we left, but got none as someone had locked
their bike to yours on the railings by the ice bin with
the Red Stripe in. You made a request – on the greenhouse
microphone – for the bike's owner to release us. I liked

the sound of your voice amplified. In this Art place
it was framed.

(You have always had an awareness of the powerful space
you hold in your mouth. It's a voice made of soft stuff but
you cut and shape your words with sharp incisive strokes
of the tongue, full lips, taut cheeks. Your words don't fall
or dribble, they are pushed out as percussion and notes.)

You were diffident on the mic. Asked the culprit to
meet you at the door. It occurred to me that there could
have been some romantic intention in the seemingly
aggressive bike-lock. Some kind of come-on? But
the owner – a person wearing shorts, trousers and a
dress all at once – would barely meet your eye.

It's just the battle for territory, you tell me, bitterly.
The claiming of space. Down to the last railing.
It's like the Wild West around here.

Soon they'll be mining the moon.

Once disentangled, you gave me a backie to the tube.
It was freezing.
My chest burned a hole in my coat.
Inside the cover, the book you had given me said

Happy new year and *happy everything.*

I couldn't make my brain understand the poetry inside,
so I tucked it down my vest.
Spread open its wings against my lungs –
An extra layer
A poultice of words
Armour?
A potion?
Your words as insulation for my breast.

By the end of the journey
I can recite every word on every page.
And I do and I do and I do and I do –
For my marriage, for my children, for my children,
an incantation of appreciation.

Excreting a welter of meanings on the cramped train,
my wrists rimy with wiped away snot bracelets
and tears secreted up my sleeve,
words burned right through the hearthole.
Cauterised.
A giant magnet on the frigidaire sky says:

Citizens!
I am simply reading all this in my heart
and writing it down!

(Dimitri Alexanych)

BODIES

Arriving home, I leave my bag in the car and take my shoes and all my clothes off at the door. Leave them in a pile on the mat. The cat slinks my bare legs as I cross the hall, pass the living room door, through which I see Mac conked out on the sofa. I take the stairs in twos, avoiding the side that creaks. In a seamless and muscular operation I remove each of my three sleeping children from their beds and carry them, one at a hot-buttered time, across the landing, nudge the door with my foot, gently swoon them down, three babies all in a line, into my own bed. The weight of each of them is, as always, entirely in proportion with the surprising strength in my arms. They pour and fold into each other and I clamber in from the pillow end. Slip in amongst the bramble of limbs. Hot legs over mine. A wandering foot pushes and kneads my thigh, into the footprint of the last time the same foot wandered over. Warm breath of sour milk and toothpaste moistens my nose. Yeasty fug of digestives, farts and marmite. I am instantly too hot and have to snatch angled breaths over all the tangle of hair in

22

my face. And I revel and swell in my discomfort. Let it radiate through me. Find a plump hand and place it on my rising ribcage. Lie there sweating, my skin sticking to theirs, sticking every inch of my skin to theirs. Proving myself a Mother.

Until it's time to get up and we all roll, shouting, wailing, whinging, pleading, into the stream of frustrations that make up a morning. Can't you just lie here asleep for ever? Must you all want things? Must you have demands and opinions and needs and feelings? Can't you just succumb to the massive authority of my love and of my need for you to be quiet and still and hot and alive but not moving, not wanting? Don't you know I was so busy last night – loving you and grieving all the seconds spent not loving you – that I haven't slept?

A million notifications appear on my phone from other mums about the potato person we are supposed to have made, ready to bring into school today. Fuck. It's potato person day. A million pics and a million lols.

Boys, eat your Weetabix / Here's one, Flo. Best I can do. / Morning. You were back late. / Why does it look like that? / Yes, you were asleep, I didn't want to wake you. / Maybe it's a person with lots of arms. They could be little hands. / He stole my spoon. / But I don't want it like that. / No I didn't. / Mummyyyyyy / What's wrong with her now? / It's potato person day. / It's what? For fuck's sake. / I don't want that one. / Where are the book bags? / I'll eat yours. / We could have done this last night. / Mummy, this is green. We are supposed to have painted them. / No you won't it's mine. / While we were hanging around waiting for you. / Give me back my spoon. / How will we make the hair? / Sorry. I forgot. / That's Flo's spoon. / I've got a sore back now. Why didn't you get me to move? / She always has the tiny one. / Maybe it's a bald person/ But I want it. / You never move. / I wanted it warm with sugar on. / But Angry Arthur has hair. / This is gross. The milk tastes funny. / You just didn't want me up in the bed. / Can't it be someone else? / I'm not taking that into school. / Snap off some of those sprouts. It could be Yoda. / I'm not going. / You never move. / I would have moved if I'd have been woken up. / My potato is stupid. / BAGS! NOW! / I'm not taking it. / I don't have time to deal with your potato. SHOES! TEETH! / Mummyyyyy / WHO HASN'T DONE THEIR TEETH? / WHY IS IT THE SAME EVERY MORNING? DO YOUR FUCKING TEETH! / There, look. It's not stupid now. It's Yoda. / That's so cool! / Mummy, Daddy's stuck a teabag / It's a cloak / We want one! / on my potato. / I'll make you one after school. / OUT. NOW. GO.

DESCENT

You are non-committal on the phone.
Say you probably won't make it to the party.

Got the winter blues I guess – a bit stuck.

I down tools.
You never not make it to a party.
You try to dissuade me:

Just thinking aloud here but isn't it kind of crazy
to come all the way here just for me? You've got
work, family, everything –

I send you some emojis.
Tell you to meet me on the platform.
And you do.

Except it's not you.

There is a figure who has stolen your coat and shadow.
Teeth and gaps and pigeon-grey, the figure barely stands
out from the concrete collage.
Who took your skin and hung there a yellowing shutter?
The man (is it a man?) holds the twisted neck
of a Sainsbury's carrier by the scruff.
Someone has worn the holes in your shoes even bigger
and worn them here.
Someone has drawn you and rubbed bits of you out.
Where are your cheeks?
Someone has stuck a pair of bitten-off lips on
and split them.

The lips say 'hey' and the arms reach around me briefly,
barely touching, and as I croon over the shoulder I smell
the hood of the coat the figure is wearing and it speaks
intensely and secretly of the secret(ion)s of your head.
Something about the smell makes the air around it
colder, like being under the covers.

Even in greeting the holey shoes don't stop moving, the
breeze keeps pushing through them, it's as though we are
fleeing, *gotta keep leaving*, too visible our breathing in the
icy air, something chased about the breaths.

I follow the figure's lead, feeling furtive.
Shoulders high, heads low we stick to the shadows as if
the avenues of Brockley are a war zone. Keep tight to the
plum trees as if their bare branches might shelter us
from missiles.

Getting to your flat feels like a break-in.
(Or rather, it felt like the execution of a lawless
routine, like dodging an alarm, deactivating a
booby trap, lowering the flag.)
As if this is a lair.

The figure strides in, defends a clamour.
Of silence.

Sidles around furniture as though it were occupied.
By fellow mute terrorists?

Empties the Sainsbury's bag onto the table as if being
hurried to lay things bare.
As if disarming.

There is a packet of Palmolive soap, a box of teabags and
a packet of couscous. The effect of these things and of the

way the figure moves around your kitchen is to emphasise the emptiness of everything. It's as though he is moving too fast through a lack of atmosphere. The incidental sounds of the chair scrape, the plastic rustle, the keys' clatter on the table, points to a paucity of conversation here.

There is a slight delay.
The sounds have been dubbed in.
The air is arid with monologue.
The strip-light strips the light of context.
Everything of detail feels superimposed.
I offer to cook but he says he's already cooked.
(Said as if there are pressing things pressing.)
I put the soap in the bathroom and it occurs to me that the soap is for me.
There has been no soap here for some time.
I had expected to clean up for you but it's already done.
The surfaces have been wiped, fingerprints smeared.
There is a piece of paper on the kitchen table –
a list turned backside up.
When he leaves the room I lift it and read in your writing:

Go for a run

Megan

Eat

Seeing my name written here in this silent and jilted place
pins me to the scene. (Implicated?)

You wrote a list, I say
(somehow honoured? – you do it too??)

I take hold of the fidgeting hands.
Look into the eyes.
They are your eyes.

I eat the lentils with the couscous.
You push yours round the plate.
The gaps between the grains feel horribly uncertain in
my mouth.
Each a tiny abyss.

EELS

It is unreasonably cold so I borrow your coat.
It's either white going gold or gold going white.
Either way it's old and has something of gold about it.
It's grubby, smells deeply of you unwashed.
I take a breath and plunge into its funk,
stuff my fists in the pockets
(where soon there will be redundant lightbulbs).
Determined.

We shift through the shadows and slip through crowds,
hunch against the wind.
I join you in the margins.

Outside Tate Modern you stop and ask barely tolerant
strangers for tobacco.
I wait for you to roll and look at the floor while I wait and
avoid their rolling eyes, I am shy.
Push on, purposeful (our only purpose to walk it through).
It's only now I realise my right ear is for listening,

the left is for hearing.
We keep swapping sides.

Waiting at the jetty for a water taxi,
we have time to kill.
Abject, ancient and tuberculoid,
the bile-green hunching sides of London
groan into the river.
The wind whips across the concrete wharf.

We slip along the shale,
absently mudlurch along the winter water's edge.
You take off your shoes (I notice you have no socks),
venture your toes into the bronze.
There used to be eels here,
but 98 % of them disappeared.
It is shocking
to see your blanched feet in the sediment and murk
of this eel-less place.
Non-biological.
Something renal, visceral, forbidden is touched.
It unnerves.
To be so close to the edge as to be in it.
Inside the edge of the threat.

It's not the water that threatens,
it's the roaring arrogance of the concrete sides.
We are krill and milt in the shadow of their crush.
Cold, metal breath chills the lungs.

In the ticket line,
you hand me a tiny glass jar with a screwed-shut lid.
Your foot found it underwater.
It is empty and has a greenish tinge.

      Thanks, I'll give it to Flo.

I hold it in my fist inside your gold-ish pocket.
Grip the thought of my daughter.
You seem oblivious to the cold.
Hard knuckles of brown water punch and bump the boat.
You walk onboard, your shoes in your hand.

STARLINGS

Night falls.
On our haunches, too taut to sit,
we squat on a bench in Brockley Park,
London's glinting context spread around us like a skirt.
I tell you about the Great Betrayal –
Birth, Motherhood, Marriage, for what it's worth.
We hold onto each others legs to steady the enormity of it all.

I put my hand in your hair and pull it like I do with
the hedges. It has turned grey.It is wiry, crisp and oily and
I secretly sniff my fingers after, and they do smell of you
of the coat of the night of the worry of the memories of a
squalor that once seemed fun but now seems symptomatic.

You keep telling me your blood is healthy, that your body
is strong, just disconnected, on its own perverse
trajectory (towards life).

Beneath the coat your clothes are clean.
You are still just a little bit vain.

34

You say the drugs are working but I don't think they are.
The gap between your front teeth is wider.
Your eyes are figs.
Your face is pleading.
There is panic in it.
I feel you slipping from my grip.
You have left it all too late:
Spent two years inventing code to emulate starlings –
flocks in flight – but forgot to watch the birds.

And deleted the sky.

You have never even met a starling.
Their numbers in the city have dropped by 87 % since
the year you were born.

> These things are true. A set of choices.
> I can't sugar cwhoat it.

That's my phrase from last night, but I swallow it and for
some reason I don't acknowledge that I recognise it and
that I am unhappy about you appropriating it.
(*I didn't* mean *for it to be put to use like that.*)
Giltcwhoated and full of throatstones
I follow you home.

SEMAPHORE

At night you switch on all the lights but mine.
Nothing will escape your neon laboratory of thought.

I leave my door open, in case you need to know I can
hear you breathing. Clatter about loudly in my room.
Go to the loo too often, making sure you know you are
not alone. Like a child at a sleepover, I name you in a
stage whisper. Not wanting to wake you, but wanting
you awake to know I am here.
Flailing about.
Trying to send a message.
Get past the dark
beyond
your naked bulbs.

In the absence of the possibility of meaningful verbal
exchange, I could lie beside you.
I call out – offer.
It comes twisting out of my mouth in somebody else's
accent.I am so far from any script at this point, I work
my way around the words through a clenched and
aching jaw.

But you decline.

The green jar you gave me is still empty.
I wish I'd phoned home.
I hold a beating starling, tight under my arm.

AND IN MY HEAD?

We lie on our backs on your sofabed. I turn off the energy-inverting lightbulb above us and reach for your hand. It is quite small, lightweight, clammy. Mine is dry and rough from too much digging. We stare up at the dark ceiling. Bach cello suites spin about our heads. This is the music I gave birth to. It played on a loop for forty-eight pupated hours. For me it is the music that reimagines time. Splits atoms. Splits body from body, self from self. To lie there motionless through all the agitation is an endurance, but I am determined. Determined you will let the endlessly self-correcting melody inch through you. Rearrange your cells. I lie there and will you to hear it out. Will it to work on your internals, muscles. Wonder if the looping phrases in some way mirror your circling thoughts. I wonder if you might find an opening and catch onto the contrapuntal shifts. Find a fractal possibility to replace your singular and ever-diminishing fifths.

I fall asleep and when I wake up you are gone.

IN THE MORNING

I lie in the clothes I slept in and remember how, making
no bones of everything, you would stand on the lawn and
chuck / wang / lob / flick the frags and stones
at the glass until I woke.

A creature, caring nothing for the wall that joined the
street to my room in the second-floor flat I shared with
your girlfriend, you would slip through the window, dust
yourself off, flick a switch.

                    The whole explodes to light.

My eyes peel in the blast but I can't see

                                        you

would have already moved on to the next room where
your girlfriend slept.

Your smile sprackles the inside of my lids,
fades to black to counting myself a sheep.
There is a word for the shape of that smile.
It says 'There it is, it's happened, it's out there and it's
outside of me, so I am just an amazed bystander like
the rest of you. What's to be done is curious but it's
not my responsibility any more than it is yours'.
What's the word for that?
~~Rueful?~~

I was happy, sandwiched there,
listing between my sheets
to the sound of you and your girlfriend fucking beyond
the wall. Adventures in motion.

I would lie there and listen:
To your pleasures
To the river below
To the trains beyond

I remember how you never came in through the door.

COFFEE IN YOUR TINY KITCHEN

Haemostasis

Biding

Sifting

Seeking the site of fracture.

X-rays of the past blink flicker and fall between us.

Tiny moments exposed in negative

dissolve into the coffee cups

as you try to explain:

you have folded yourself a paper bird,

each faultline / precrease a dehiscence,

so that you are a scaffold of wounds –

a relief of *old* pain.

You push your soft voice out of a tight space in your
mouth when you speak, to **p**uncture, to **p**unctuate, to
emphasise the **r**elentless **r**hythm of it, the **i**mpossibly
small **s**pace of it, the **v**iolence of it, the **u**nfairness of it,
since **you deserve the same as everyone else**.
As though someone took from you, someone came and

41

stole decision from you, someone robbed your liberty to move from you and held you down to the torture chair, under the bulb, to go over and over how **Freedom is overrated**, in your lucky-to-have-it flat.

thenowirrelevantflat
thenowirrelevantfoodinthefridge
thenowirrelevantkettle
Schreeeeeeeeeeeeeeeeeeeeeeeeeeeeeeeeeeeeeeeeeeeeeeeeeeee
eeeeeeeeeeeeeeeeeeeeeeeeeeeeeeeeeeeeeeeeeeeeeeeeeeeeeeeee
eeeeeeeeeeeeeeeeeeeeeeeeeeeeeeeeeeeeeeeeeeeeeeeeeeeeeeeee
eeeeeeeeeeeeeeeeeeeeeeeeeeeeeeeeeeeeeeeeeeeeeeeeeeeeeeeee
eeeeeeeeeeeeeeeeeeeeeeeeeeeeeeeeeeeeeeeeeeeeeeeeeeeeeeeee
eeeeeeeeeeeeeeeeeeeeeeeeeeeeeeeeeeeeeeeeeeeeeeeeeeeeeeeee
eeeeeeeeeeeeeeeeeeeeeeeeeeeeeeeeeeeeeeeeeeeeeeeeeeeeeeeee
eeeeeeeeeeeeeeeeeeeeeeeeeeeeeeeeeeeeeeeeeeeeeeeeeeeeeeeee
eeeeeeeeeeeeeeeeeeeeeeeeeeeeeeeeeeeeeeeeeeeeeeeeeeeeeeeee
eeeeeeeeeeeeeeeeeeeeeeeeeeeeeeeeeks

You leap up
and turn it off.

DESK

I am sitting at your desk, calling Mac, conveying too-late details and assurances about when I will be home.

The desk is strewn with sticky notes and diagrams. A kind of map shows a tracing of your movements between the flat, the tube station, the arts centre where you work and the shop. The pencil lines have been drawn over again and again, so as to wear away a tear in the paper. Diminished coordinates. Tight, synaptic looping. Constellation of pain. You have tried to gain a bird's eye view. (I always thought you were tapping at the glass to get out, but you told me last night that you were still just trying to get in.)

The map shows your animal architecture. The innate practices and routines, the weave of your life. It is an attempt to escape your narrative. To lay yourself out in your bare bones. But the picture's loop looks like a noose. A snare. A bear trap in the bed.

43

There is an angled lamp with another glaring bulb in it,
poised ready to strike. There are some beautiful things
(the deep anatomy of a flower, scratched onto beach-
glass), and some things that speak of your former self
(a complex, self-made modular sound-rack, a machine
with a thousand strands of wire connecting the corners
of the universe through infinite reverb).

There is a pot with a sapling plum in it, fostered from
the tree that pushes up the tarmac outside your window.
The soil is parched.

Under the desk is a pair of newish trainers, with no holes
in the toes. It occurs to me that you have made a choice
to wear the holey ones. Just as you choose to cadge
tobacco from strangers or pick butts from the floor.
That this is saying something you wish to say.

I remember how you are never accidental, but you are
always right in the blur of things. And in the spaces
between beats. The build before the release. The place
where possibility lies. Occupying the blanks. I am
struck by the danger in that. The risk that you might
fall through.

Yes Mac, I will be home in time for tea. Did you remember about swimming? Her goggles? OK, OK. Sorry, I know you do. I know. Of course I'll bring them presents. I'll be there to put them to bed. Yes I do love you too. I love you too.

BACK HOME

Space is fiercely carved.
Against the grain of the meat.

I'm sorry I forgot the presents.

(u frgot Flo's jar: still on shelf
Shit. cringe emoji.)

Sorry sorry sorry sorry. Yes, I know I promised.
You go out. Get some time for yourself. I agree.
It's only fair.

There's the physical space (rubble that gets pushed
around in little piles from one side of our house to
the other), there's the mental space (hahaha!) and
the *shared space.*

(youbreatheIbreatheyoubreatheIbreatheyoubreatheI-
breathe, remember?)

46

Scratting catshit off the hem of our draft-excluding
curtains and eventually giving up and trimming them
with scissors (they are getting shorter and shorter – how
does she do it? She must be shitting upwards), I mourn
all that wide-open space we spent.

All those blank tapes, squandered.

Blissfully ignorant were we that soon the sky would be
full of drawing pins and little flags.

That every silence would be gated.

I carve out a new space.
A sliver.
Family time.

INVITATION

For fuck's sake.

I know. I'm sorry. Kids?! Put your bags by the door!

You always make it so I'd be a cunt to say no. That's how you keep control

Now, please kids! And do your wees. We're leaving in five minutes! / You fucking plan something for once. I'd fucking love you to take control.

No you wouldn't you'd fucking hate it.

No I wouldn't I'd fucking love it.

OK, I'm telling you Kit can't come on our fucking family holiday.

Fuck off.

EATING ECLAIRSES ON THE A40

Boys? Flo? There's something you need to know.
Remember Kit? My friend? Our friend?

No. / Yes. / No.

He's coming on holiday with us.

Cool! / Why? / Oh.

Dad's going to pick him up from the station when we
get there.

Am I? / Ok. / Oh. / Why? / Am I?

He's not very well.

Oh. / Ok. / Why? / It's a two-hour trip.

He's not being sick or anything. He's just not feeling
great.

Why? / Oh, ok. / Can I have an eclair please? /
Fuck's sake.

So I want you all to just be really nice to him, show him
that we love him and that we care about him and make
him feel welcome, ok?

Mum? / Why? / Why? / Jesus.

And don't ask him loads of questions. He might not want to talk about it.

Ok. / Why? / Eclairses!

Promise?

Thanks. / We want one too. / Yeah.

Told you they'd be fine with it.

It's fine. I just don't want him there. Give us an eclair. Stop hogging them.

I'm not.

Just know that. I'll put up with it, but I don't want it.

It won't be so bad.

He's gone mental. He'll be mental in front of the kids.

He won't be.

He'd better fucking not be.

Or what?

Or you can all fuck off.

COTTAGE

This is a characterful Welsh holding cottage that offers two reception rooms, both with open fires, and a kitchen diner overlooking the pond and guarding. Upstairs are four bedrooms (two doubles and two singles). Bed linen is provided, but please bring your own trowels.

SWING ELEGY

Three children tear a strip from the picture,
rip down the centre of the road,
bowl over a moss of piled slate,
a crippled gate.
They slide inside the ferns, black rocks
where there is a rope swing.

She's first in!

Frock with a strawberry print
skims froth off the stream's sprint.
With each push across the gargling maw

More!

white cotton of skirt withdraws,
gauze releases sepals,
flattened petals
thumb the water

Woooaaahhh!

Spring's brochure:
flick-book of light
pendulum of flight

Daring daughter
Daring daughter
Daring daughter

Flo!

There's a game of pirates.
She's up in the rigging,
while on the slick and gleaming decks
two boatswains busy digging
sift for specks of gold.
Fists of river grit
turn and fold spring's glinting plunder.

Dredged, the skirt now drips, sticking wet, itches the legs.
The twins have marked their spot.
NeXt
Three scythes are drawn from branches
of what trees Mac would know.
Smacking bracken,
tracking the pattern of other kids' skips, whacks and kicks,
meadowver heels home.

Fight me! Fight me! I won't go violent!

As we near the top the picture's silent, fixed,
sucked behind us, stilled.

I nurse my pleasure.
The jam or country wine I make
Of this precious time coagulates,
claims summer's straining sun
and fills a demijohn with spring's sweet promise.
Tonic against dread.
It knocks against my ribs.
Hope clamps the lid.
Catalogue idyll.

The car is visible in the drive.
On arrival all three fall upon the creaking door,
wetting the shadowy walls,
stripped-open hearts and naked greetings
pour in.

Men shuffle and shrink back, the tide retreating.
Mac to his beer in the kitchen, fags at the door,
smoke hanging in the air from our unfinished war
and still in the hall, tugging wellies –

We heard you're sick / we hope you feel better / want
to watch telly?

Noise crashes unabashedly past.
Fills the house.
Light, sound, weight of alive life
lurches you into your new circumstance,
pushes you upstairs as flotsam in a flooded home,
adrift.
The bottle I am armed with, brim with message,
gives short shrift, drains within seconds,
is absorbed by the black sponge and fissure
you cannot iFx, your deepened winter.
You are bird without feathers, tree without leaves, skeletal.
I show you to your room in the eaves
and you retreat all pinched, apologetic.

> Aw this is so kind but you know I'm not sure it's going to
> work. I shouldn't be here, you know I'm kind of a state.

> It's alright. Honest. I'll bring you something to eat,
> as tea will be a while.

You recoil.
Hole up in the hull.
Trying not to find your discomfort hurtful
I reach out and touch you, careful,
but you cower inside your cradle of riddles,

while the three little kiddles huddle on the sofa,
missing the matinée showing of suffering (I hope)
and watching *The Simpsons* instead.

I slope off to the kitchen,
where Mac's making a meal of things.
A glass of wine (red).
Wife and husband sink back to what norms
we are accustomed these days.
We whisper storms and batter at the bilge strakes,
tear chunks out of love-wormed rinds,
thrash out some lines of the argument.
Our surly mouths slack with tannin,
we're still at it: chewing each other over.
Sicktothebackteeth.

Slowly drunker
we hunker down and drown each other out.
Flouting sense we guzzle all the words
until

     KIT?

     KIDS?! Would you give him a shout?
Supper is served.

AROUND THE TABLE

Mac tells jokes.
I honey the heel of the bread.
Coax you into eating, speaking.
The kids rattle the box of questions:

> What is a solar plexus?
> When will we go nocturnal?
> Where does Jesus get the chocolate?

We laugh, or at least expel some air.
We pass the salt.
Maybe this can work if we let it?

Did you know that Kit's a photographer? And
he's writing a kind of a book. He could help you with
your homework. He used to sell real gold – actual bars
of gold – on the internet. Nothing to do with the banks.
Like a sort of pirate. Tell them, Kit. He's a great goalie.
And he's really good at chess. Maybe he would teach you?

This will all be ok.
There are details left after all.
Our chests click into place.

                                        Oh yeah?

Words whir and billow gently round us.
Ideas are passed carefully, from hand to mouth.
Small mercies, nothing is spilled.
The words settle.
They keep coming and they keep settling
and as we talk,
from a crack in the ceiling above our heads
a gentle snow of meanings begins to fall.
(As late as April?!)
At first we catch them on our tongues and in our ears
but they fall faster, faster, weightless falling, faster

they fall,

    fall

covering the dinner plates

    drifting against the table legs

                    blueing our ears

                            numbing our lips

slowly we slur our words

        quieter and quieter our sounds are heaped over

            with soothing snow.

It slows our breathing

walls up the windows

                    fills all the spaces

      with cataracts

settles our sense of normal.

Holds us, cold and close

blind and biding our time.

PHOTOGRAPHS

There are old black and white family portraits on the mantelpiece. There's something out of place about them. Somehow they don't fit.

You and Mac marvel at the incongruity and the unexpectedness of this obviously foreign, obviously bookish couple with their bespectacled children in this rural Welsh hamlet slash dead-end street.

For Mac this is a bit of banter. A distracting game. But you have become quite invested in their story. You keep hovering over the fireplace, where you roll spindly rollies and peer into the frames, as if looking for small print.

On the wall there is one of those aerial photographs. The cottage. Garden. Pond. A parked car. Two crumpled piles of brown clothing with people in, sit on a bench out front. It's barely possible to make them out at all, but you compare them – the tiny old couple on the bench, with the young monochrome couple in the portraits. It has to be them! Years later! You can tell! The man, especially. You can see it! See it around the mouth and chin.

I think it's pretty obvious the holiday cottage company just bought the photographs on the mantel along with the other knickknacks and bits and bobs from some flea market. Dotted them around to give it that homely, rustic feel. They have nothing to do with this place or the two slack smudges in the aerial shot, thousands of feet below. But I don't say anything. Don't want to burst this small bubble. It's as though it escaped the mincing grid of your depression. As if, for a moment, a tiny part of your mind forgot itself and this little innocent, imaginative flatulence squeezed out. Weightless and oblivious and floating free.

EMPATHY

Front stage, you chat with Mac,
play chess with the kids,
pretty breezy.

                    He doesn't seem too bad to me.

But backstage, at me you desperately snatch,
prise apart my days

                    – slide in asides –

snare me in a secret
net of urgent whispers.
The dense web of your workings-out.

Your pressing voice presses.
Leaves its imprint all over me.
A sub-plot that bruises my vision
splits all my moments lengthways,
fills my eyes with your flat gratuitous light.

I feel my way forward cautiously.
Conscious of blundering.
Fearful of some unseen tipping point –
of showing alarm, which may alarm you,
of showing a lack of alarm, which may alarm you.

My face stiffens.
My fibres thicken.
I wooden.

Meanwhile the 'real' conversation continues,
demands of me a bodily presence.
The familiar cycles (liquids in / liquids out)
insist I take a stance,
engage with the physically irrefutable things:

> What do you call a rock that floats? (A log)
> What do you call a dog with no legs? (A log)
> What do you call a dog? (Bumface)

I find all the answers between gritted teeth.

My surfaces repel.

I'm the hollow rock from the joke.

Petrified.

Caught between the wild horizon and the muddy stolid shore.

And every time Mac reaches,

briny displacement sends me lurching, adrift,

further, farther? further out.

NOISES / (IN)FERTILE CONDITIONS

Bach cello suites again.

The fire is crackling very loudly.

You eat nearly all the chocolate eggs.

Your fingers are feverish for them –

scrabbling and snatching –

a cuckoo's clutch almost,

since they are really meant for the children.

You devour them.

Some kind of chemical absorption.

I feel at once repelled and deeply tender,

as I sometimes felt about my breastfeeding babies.

There is something cruel about the garishness of the

egg shapes.

Ectopic foil fugazis.

Lurid little abortions.

You keep pushing air out of your lungs very loudly. It is

almost percussive, along with the crackling fire and the

agitating of the foil eggs against the wooden bowl
very loudly.

I understand that this incessant non-speech is torturous
for Mac, and the music with no obvious direction, and the
insistent what he calls sighing reminding him painfully of
the Black Moods from his childhood: the incredible
smothering weight of it. The knowing that *Some*body's
brooned aff.

But I resist the temptation to make things more
comfortable by breaking the rhythm in the room,
or disturbing the air.

The decision not to rescue
wields some kind of oppression
– the weight of the noise –
I let it smother us.
And in the same moment I am bent on resuscitation,
bending over you with blinkers on,
mothering you with a kiss of life
for which I forgot to ask your consent.

I nudge the tower the kids have made with my toe.
Magnetic applause brings down the house.
The smashed moment gives you your exit.
Propelled by an adrenaline I can taste
you take off and go to your room.

I put the blocks of colour back in their box and feel like a
bully, ashamed.

PILLOW TALK

I knew it would be like this.

Like what?

Your neck's all tight. It's supposed to be a holiday.

It is a holiday. I'm fine.

You're not fine.

It was an emergency. Is an emergency.

There's always some emergency.

What else was I supposed to do? His brother's gone away.

I know.

Just be nice to him.

I am being nice to him. Of course I am.

He's ill.

I know he's fucking ill.

Take him fishing or something.

Yeh fucking great.

Thanks.

Don't thank me.

Why?

Because I'm not taking him fishing for you. I'm not doing any of it for you. I'm doing it for him. It's not your thing to thank me for.

Ok.

Don't roll your eyes at me.

You can't even see my eyes!

You are rolling your eyes at me and making me out to be an unreasonable cunt. I'll take him fishing. I'll hang out with him. I'll do whatever he wants. It's not him I'm cross with. It's you – it's you who's the cunt here.

Fuck you.

Fuck you too.

FROM WHEN YOU JUMPED IN THE SEA / BLOODBATH

Overnight,
somebody plugged you and turned on the taps.
Visible, mineral, chemical fear
rising like sap, adrenaline at its purest
is crawling up inside your dermis,
around your body is visibly surging
something caustic, burning for an exit.
You are snared in there.
So you get up sit down.
Get up sit down get up sit down get up.
Your movements are jerky, on limited elastic.
You commit to breaking out,
pecking your locks.
Lancing elbows, forehead, the underside of your knees,
all a peeled bare.
You have tethered yourself here to your laptop,
but your mind keeps making a run for it and you can't

clot it, stop it battering round your cramped little skull.
Mac strides in (as requested),
suggests we go out for a stroll,
maybe fly a kite? Walk on the cliffs,
fight the brave sea, even.

You acquiesce but leaving sight of the laptop is tough.
It's a source of pain like the clawed-at skin.
This has become your grip on things, your horizon.

The sky is another screensaver.
It waits for us patiently
as we all pick our way down to the shore,
our poor procession of winter legs
mincing and snipping the spring air like pinking shears.
Ribbons of words (mainly mine) straggle behind us
in the bare blue breeze.

Three kids in front clatter spades
on the white pebbled path.
Mac, fishing net aloft,
and you, sloping slowly away, last,
drawn to the crest of the earth
where the scree skips three steps into the swelling thirst.

Once we've hit the beach
the kids chase and kick the horses,
run away shrieking.
Mac and I race it, double-daring –
there's nothing for it but to strip.
Cock cupped, tits gripped,
one-legged stalk stance,
untangle of socks and pants,
elbows jutting, we cut and chuck away our modesty.
The children cheer,
you stand quietly apart.

There is a terrible sharpness to it,
a splicing of breath.
The awful ache and shrink.
But I am robust.
Screaming is inevitable,
affirming something.
Mac howls to the surface, lurches, scarpers,
swears acres for his blue murdered mollusc,
cracks up the kids in stitches.
I brave it out.
Coddle my heartbeat.
Breathe through a grille of numbers –

In-two-three, out-two-three, in——

All osmosis, giving it up,
until I'm sure I've won.

As I am pulling myself back together again,
the stiffness in my animated body tells me this is
somehow a demonstration of joy –
How to live and feel!
It's not real. Or at least, it's all for your benefit.
Mac knows it too, though I think for him this
represents success –
There, that's how you do it! (tick!)
And there's a deliberate disinterest in consent –
We know what's best for you / it's for your own good!

I wrap in towels, sit shivering on a rock.
Barnacles bite my arse, as I pretend to read,
watch over the top of the page,
as you stand at the edge of the deep trench where the
stream meets the sea.

There is no joy in you as fully clothed, you leap.
Just determination to fight reluctance.
You barely draw breath.
In one stroke you chop the legs off
our naked little pantomime.
Knock it flat.

There is a conflict of water and air.
It is brutal, but you come up silent.
Stand and drip on the stones.
Your hollow chest heaves.
There is nothing to share.
Even when you are smashed apart
you are still con/detained.
Unreached
Unable to give
Unable to give us your sound.

With rictus lips
you play rescue with the kids on the rocks.
I wonder if they notice your smile
is detached from the rest of you.
That when jumped you sliced through something.
That what came out was skin only.

They think they are making you better,
and the game is proof it's working.
I think Mac thinks this too:
(Want to go fishing later?)
I think he thinks he's / we're (?) winning.

When I went to get the towels from the car,
sat with the radio for a moment's leave,
there was a feature on the Faroe Isles.
A whale cull.
Bloodbath.
Interviews with ~~onlookers~~ witnesses –
a violence unimaginable.

Seawater clicks in my ears.

WHILE WE ARE ASLEEP

Kit creeps out,
lifts the latch.
A pressure valve released
causes us to sleep deeper
through dawn
as he hops it, over the hedge and down the road.
Towards the beach.

No sign.
No note.

> Kit?
> KIT?
> *For fuck's sake.*

We set to trawling the lanes.
High hedges limit the view.
Obstinate blackthorns
stricken with what-ifs
snag us as we search.

We can't call you.
The stubborn, signal-less sky is thick with deafness.
We resort to shouting.
Split off in different directions,
frayed with fear.

Mac revisits the cliff where you recently flung the lobster
pot, fashioned from a shopping basket and a washing line,
in a moment of focused inspiration characteristic of a
character we once knew.

I consider dialling 999.
Stand at the sink
shucking my heart,
along with all the other muscles.
Until the boys appear,
flanking you, two small bodies
steer you home unquestioning,
as I tear at you with questions
and vacant, you leave us filling in the blanks.

My heart sits purging
in the washing-up bowl.
Spitting out the grit.

CRISIS

I am out in the field MENTAL HEALTH PLEASE
HOLD at the back of the garden, on the ridge NO,
NOT A DANGER TO OTHERS, NO where there
are two bars of signal when there is no wind. PLEASE
HOLD. The sky is the blue-dark of lengthening dusk.
I have to shout NO THERE IS NO A&E SITUATION
to be heard above the poor reception PLEASE HOLD
making garish bunting of your most intimate laundry.
NO THERE IS NO INJURY. THERE IS A RISK.
AN ONGOING RISK OF INJURY. Ewes NOTHING?
NOTHING YOU CAN DO? loudly seek their lambs
somewhere over the hedge. NOTHING. THANK YOU.

SHARKS

We have found a stack of sun loungers in the shed,
snapped the off-season rust from the joints,
dragged them onto the lawn.

Having created a pleasing mise-en-scène of easy compan-
ionship and leisure, we lie back (bit chilly?) with books.

I am reading an anthology that keeps picking me up and
putting me down again. You have chosen some junk from
the shelf in the bathroom here, having failed to pack
anything of your own.

Mac missioned off early with the kids, to look for great
white sharks.

(Daddy, are the sharks real? / Two were spotted here last
year alone! / Mum, aren't you coming? / Why would you
come to a place as exciting as this and spend your whole
time with your face in a book you could look at anywhere?
They want you to come. *I want* you to come.)

We lie there, necks bent, eyes running over,
cover to cover, absorbing nothing.
The book goes up, the book goes down.

You begin to pick and peck again,
at ragged tufts of theories / greenery.
You worry the earth,
turn over endless pebbles
in search of worms, warmth, words.
Drawn in, I make suggestions,
list your options,
lay them out like milk-bottle tops
(shiny! silver! full-fat!) along a wall.
Pray for spring chicks / some feasible beginning
to hatch from the incubation tray
I have plugged into the sky's dangling socket.

I have a sense that if we breathe on it
Speak to it in the right coaxing tones
Touch its buttons in combinations we don't yet know
Give it a sly wank

It will yield, if not a new life,

then some kind of therapeutic conclusion –

A message

A shaft of an idea

A home

A cool hand

Half a stroke of a songline?

A slow spray of moss up your walls.

But all about us pile dismissed possibilities

Embryos spoiled

Things gone cold, overlooked

Laid clinical waste.

We've put down our books and we are now knee-deep

in the husks of words.

(Words! When we could be out hunting for sharks!)

       Aw, I know but—

       It's just I'm kind of—

       I just can't see past—

       There's just no—

     (So many ways of saying the same thing.)

In the face of nothing I offer you everything,
plead with you to see:

That you need to practise pretending
Until it becomes habitual
That I will do it with you – I can take it
That I have room for a lot of blood –
I could be your Mooncup…?
That you can have whatever I have got
That you are still pretty fucking hot
There are plenty of fish / Other jobs / Other cities /
Other fields
You could come and live with us!
Paint out house
Dig the garden
Write a book!
Borrow the kids!
Borrow me
I could be your surrogate
I have so much – too much love to manage
You can take it. Share it at least. Here. Take it. TAKE IT.
Would you fucking well take it?
Take something? Please?
You fucking mindfuck.

(Yes, this is a mindfuck, only you are watching the
telly or gazing out the window over my shoulder and
miming hollow sounds while I am frotting away.
Frotting at impossible possibilities, flightless fantasies that
leave you untouched.)

With each word my intestines jerk upwards
and out my throat.
I am a sausage machine of rejected ideas.
Until I have listened / listed myself empty.
Spent.
Shark bait going cold.

SWAGBAGS

When the others get back from the expedition
we are still sitting stiff, in the same positions,
our books still propped open at the same page.

> We didn't find any sharks / Are you sure they exist
> Mummy? / But we did find cockles and there are
> millions of them!! We are going to eat them for tea
> tomorrow! / Where is tea? / Haven't you cooked?

                                        Sorry, I forgot.

Everyone's starving. I thought you might have nipped
to the shop? We've been gone all day!

                                        Didn't think.

Right, kids, let's cook these cockles now then, shall we?
We can wash them in the bath. Flo, you and Kit go
and turn the taps on.

Water rushes. AC/DC blasts.
(It's a dog-eat-dog. Eat cat too.)
Kids elbow-deep in teamwork.
Simple instructions are issued.

> Kit, look in the glovebox of the car. There's some
> cheese in there from on the way here.
> We can have it for afters.

We open the cheese and it's full of maggots.
Tiny ones. Unborn, white, blind.
The whole wedge ripples and squirms with them.
They disperse over the kitchen counter.
A stop-motion animation of something melting.
Mac reckons the maggots must be 99 % cheese.
Together you quickly decide you will eat the maggots.
It is a thrill to be so alive and eating maggots together.
The maggots taste of cheese.
Together you marvel at your audacity.
At the pull between revulsion and curiosity.
At the immolation of boundaries.

Your laugh is tugging the joke up from your gut in
short   sharp   jerks –

One, two, three!

　　　You unify in the swallowing.

When you laugh you sound like a seal.
You vocalise the inbreath,
not the exhale and release
There is a hinge in it, a knack to it.
Over the years I have learned to listen for the
lock click – like sneaking out after hours.
It's a felt ritual made of sound and touch,
since turning the light on would alert the grownups.
Where it opens wider than a jar, that's the moment.
The rush.
Now!
The moment is stolen.
The laugh is all in your lungs.
Swagbags of air.
We all want some of that.
I hang back, watching. In awe.
Borrow Mac. Borrow him.

He's the one that knows about living.
He can live for us all.

Mac who can skin a rabbit without a knife
Mac who is a genuinely impressive ballet dancer
Mac who makes friends with all the grannies
Mac who loves my armpit hair and body odour
Mac who can play a kazoo like a flugelhorn
Mac who is (still) happy to have sex on my period
Mac who kisses the cat on the lips
Mac who shouts when he's angry
Mac who cries when he's sad
Mac who gets drunk because he enjoys it
Mac who shits out shiny song lyrics
Mac who knows the value in hunting imaginary sharks
Mac who knows where his bread is buttered
Mac who says sorry when he's sorry
And doesn't when he's not

I go upstairs and close the door.

IN SPITE

I'm sorry.

And we do fuck and I do think – I can't help but think – that maybe from me (not from Mac this time), *maybe* from me, this is a performance too. Another demonstration of pleasure. And I wonder if the noise of it – the animal, unthinking, day-to-day togetherness of it – reaches you beyond the wall. And I can't help but question whether there is a tiny pinch of cruelty in the sounds I'm making.
(Adventures in motion.)

Mac falls asleep and I turn over the pillow and avoid the wet patch on the sheet: cold guilty salt in the wound. I know you are awake. You are always awake. And I know you can sense the mess and clutter of our deeply, painfully, roughly lived lives pressing on you from all sides. Our blood is hot. Our blood is thick. There is no water in our blood. There is no water in our blood.

I push a note under the door with my mind.

I'm sorry.

I'm sorry.

You were right. You shouldn't be here.

POTION

We are on the patio, baked in evening sun.
I am peeling potatoes.
You and Flo are making shapes,
sprawled on the black slate.
It is warming her tummy, she says,
she likes it.

You are belly up, propped on elbows,
head hanging on its hinge.
For me you are barely there,
but with Flo there is some minimal exchange.
She's lost her ball, she's bored,
strips flowers off twigs of dried up thyme,
sings scraps of ditties and half-formed rhymes
for you to catch and do what you like with.
These don't just bounce off you, you angle a return
(like directing shards of sunlight with a watch face).
Idly, you pick up her rhythm,
casually chuck back some words,
playing but at the same time playing it down,

90

so that it's not giving with the thought and effort of a present,
it's a shrugging off, an easy gesture.
Giving without sacrifice. (Why not?)
Because what you have to give is yourself
and yourself is without worth and it just happens to be there,
~~unwrapped~~ detached.

Flo *loves* and sees you as fair game.
She is up to the challenge.
She is determined to DETERMINE everything,
in the way she does – wanting a puppet.
She has one in me. (A straw-headed stiff thing on a pole,
craving *time to think* with the sprouting spud of
BOREDOM in my brain hole).

You are not worn down by *fun*.
Maybe it lifts you?
You are available for the yes let's.

Oh yeah?… Ok.

You are hers. (Why not?)
While I am too busy twisting on my pole (frothing the air, in
an effort to feel efficient, flapping my arms at the gulls that
worry my barren fieldful of personal space).

Her chatter becomes a chant,

becomes some kind of spell.

The need for a potion emerges.

Mummy says you are sick but you don't look sick to me.

         Oh yeah? What do you think I look then?

Just like a person really.

         Oh yeah?

What do you need to make you better?

Kit needs a wife, I interject,

trying to protect my daughter from the depths,

and in the process sacrificing the weight of the problem.

But she shrugs – Oh, Ok.

The task is beneath her.

She toils away at the tincture.

Leads a forage from which a recipe concocts, as each

find is dropped – plip – into my pan of spuds.

He is her sous, her apprentice.

They amble off to look for an eggcup,

the vessel for the ritual.

I can hear her chuntering instructions

and him reaching for the high shelves.

Childsize flip flops plapping
on the cool shaded tiles
of the kitchen floor.

Alone now I peel.

Their patter patching a picture of patched together plans,
the barest of story bones,
slung together with improvisational ease.

They are still making shapes
with ideas that shift and shake and
dance out through the open kitchen window,
buoyed and bobbing along on a breeze of calypso classics,
playing from a phone – an algorythmic reminder
that we are all here to HAVE A GOOD TIME.

(Calypso…)

Choose a colour for your wife, what do you think? Pink?

(resistance)

But, my favourite is pink, so…

(resistance)

Yes, but I think she would like the same as me, so we'll have pink, Ok? Ok. So.

(gives in)

It's for you to get married, so we need to get things to make it taste nice…

(Calypso…)

Personal spacing

All this space

Mac is out fishing

The boys are down the stream

The sun is low in the evening windows

The sun is in the pan.

Drifting, I am drawn to its surface

Hoping my reflected face will reflect some hope

I peer and poke at the potion

And in a mindslip

       – a wish

I am fished in.

I plunge first my crown, my Mothers' Crown.
(Star of fast-fading colour / saxifrage.)
And then the rest.

Bodily, I break the water,
which is not water but liquid dream.
My mind swims into the potion and its belief.
Above, the hole of sky –
a circle tone of a singing bowl tuned the notes of
MEEEE (I think it's Dsharp/G).
Below, Flo's ingredients.
An assemblage of symbols and signs,
both divine and throw away at once:

> Pebbles from the beach
> Flowers of thyme
> Lego blocks
> A beer bottle top
> Hairband
> Marble
> Cloves
> Lemon pips
> Potato peel
> Tiny balls of Easter-egg foil

A shiny glittering sticker
Each a sacrament
God's vajazzles.

Skulling low,
I find I have no need of air.
And although I can hear the world up there,
it's far away and cut free as birds over the sea.
A universe removed.

All about me, personal space.
All about me, bright, bewildering everything.

HANDS I SEE, COULD BE MINE
LEGS AND FEET I SEE, COULD BE MINE,
WHAT WEARING? BOOBS? All abobbing.

I float
Full
Funning
Submerged in a tincture from another world away.
From a time before the existence of lists:

A time before we learn to colour inside the lines.
A time of **100% starlings** and **100% eels**.

From a time when anything that comes to hand
becomes anything that comes to mind.

From a time when we are shorter and therefore
closer to things that smell of bracken.
When friendships don't just linger, they happen.

From a time when things are not always joined to words
and potions are everyday solutions.

Until I am sucked back into focus
as close up
Flo's golden eye
Fills my sky

Mummy! Mummy?

and in a blink
I am back beside them,
snatched suddenly out of the pan, looking in.

Mummy, do you think we have everything we need?

She doesn't wait for an answer.
She is already setting the eggcup on the ceremonial slate,
carefully laying a sugar spoon
(she has a thing for tiny spoons (who doesn't)),
by the side of the egg goblet.
She is fussing over the ornaments,
tiny woman-wrists frothing the air.
Kit is hovering, mind on God / who / Christ knows what,
and it's then I thrust out my hands as though catching a
baby —
Snatch
Grasp
Draw towards lips
Gulp.

I want *more* —
The brightness
The weightless fun
The liquid gold of the time when / the time before…

Mummy! That's for Kit! Mummy!

Gulp gulpgulp.

(Down set the goblet.)

Sorry. (Sleeve wipes smile off face) Sorry.

Kit it's your turn. (Pretend Mummy didn't do that.)
Mummy, it's for Kit's wife. That's what we made it for.

Sorry.

(Small pearl of burp.
Pleasure repeats.)

Hic.

Sorry.

MAYFLIES

The others have already moved on to the next thing,
rescuing the football from the middle of the luminous
green patch called a pond.

In an effort to reach it with a stick, they have pushed it
further out.

They are very far away.

The taste of magic still plays on my lips.
All that personal space has unfurled inside me.
The underworld of colour has blurred my vision beyond
the patterns of recognition and sense.

I can no longer find the edges of myself.

I watch as tiny bits of matter or is it krill or flying
creatures see me dispersed and soluble, a murmuration of
cells with no centre.

The potatoes in the pan are potatoes again and I am pretty sure I am not a potato too, but there are other distinctions I can't be so certain of.

Time, for example. Then, now and when – seem to have folded in on themselves. Much as Flo's body is folded against the air around her as she leans over the pond.

Kit is holding the back of her dress so she can retrieve the ball. The stretched-taut dress is like a pink curtain and the sound is of a curtain dropped. A kind of curtain crumpling sound. And the slime is impossibly green and her dress is abhorrently pink, baby pink.

I can see midges ... mayflies ... suspended.

And there is a clapping.

A mighty applause sound rushing down my ear canals. It's the sound of a roaring circus trick, a fabulous disappearing act that has hatched itself inside my skull. It is running down the walls of my mind like a cold shot of that drug they offer you in your birth plan and you refuse (so naïve, woman), but end up having anyway. A shot of sheer and icy removal as they push the needle that blocks you, push as the baby is coming and all that will matter is baby – you will not care about your murdered self your murdered self will not matter – your matter will be subsumed by baby. Baby will be your everything (forget the definite article making baby separate and singular), baby will appear and you will disappear. Baby is not separate, baby is your world

Baby is –

Baby has – ?

Baby has disappeared from view completely, from sound completely, from in front of mummy and left a clamouring in mummy's icy spine. The world is luminous green, the world is mucous thick, thick viscous time, the world is screaming get her out get her out get her out and Kit is just standing there. He's just standing there, he's just standing, he's just standing there, he's just standing there unwrapped. In front of Mummy Kit stands over where there is no baby.

My skull is curetted clear.

Tear through personal space
Splice of cold
Cold scrabbling blackness
Horribly soft fronds
Fucking fronds
Thick soup of pond
Gropen sunken prayers
Grope and part apart
No colour
No sound
No sound
No baby

Frond Hair Scalp Eyesocket Armpit Body Baby?
Body.
Push
Gasp
Surface
Kit?!
Smothering my view as he bends closer in
The screaming hole of his mind
    A hand outstretched.

Haul.
Baby. Mummy.
Green afterbirth
The world squirms with umbilica
All the long songs all the short songs
All the spaces all the eggs
Calypso calypso caypso calypso
I breatheyoubreatheIbreatheyoubreatheIbreatheyoubreathe,
remember?
Pump pump pump pump
His mouth is a green tunnel
Push push push push
Her mouth is a black crab
IbreatheyoubreatheIbreatheyoubreathe

Her skin is moonskin blue

Pushpushpushpush

Calypso calypso calypso calypso

Cough

Retch

Wrench

From the space hole she is cut

Gouged out

Flung life

Flung lungs   fill fill fill

She is shrunk-wrapped in the pink meaning

Laminate in my mummyness

She sicks up a salamander

A heron swings by and swallows it whole

The moon slips a little

Eyes brim with blood.

Together,

wrapped tight as tubes

we warm inside.

Watch out the window of the settling night,

let your Kit's shape dissolve

slowly,

fade and lose its name.

RESPONSE

It's not responsible. No, you were not being responsible: he's not *responsible*. We have a responsibility. *They* are our responsibility. This is totally irresponsible. It would be the responsible thing to do. We're not responsible. Who is responsible? Whose responsibility is he?

EASTER

You look like a crim hunched in the passenger seat
when we wave you off.
Your eyes are animals.
A look that reminds me of the relief
in giving up on choice.
Mac looks grim at the wheel.
The boys just stand, on the upstairs landing.
Flo's on my hip.
A light overnight rain
has lifted the rosemary smell from the bush at the gate,
gives the air the fresh, medicinal taint
of slaughtered lambs.
You know what you have to do.
We wave until we can't hear the engine anymore.

ISCK

The kids are being sick all over the house.
The place stinks.
I've opened every window.

In a text you tell me you think it's you —
your sickness infecting us.

> Of course it wasn't you. It's a bug.
>
> Sorry.
>
> Are you home yet?
>
> no. cnt go.
>
> Why?
>
> ?
>
> Thought you were going to hosp? Or back to dr?
>
> Scrd: 2 brutal.
>
> Where are you now?
>
> On train still. gng to sctlnd.
>
> Where? Why?
>
> Glsgw.

What? You ok?

Thumbs-up emoji

Who you with? You should be with your bro.

Busy.

Your mum then.

Same.

Shouldn't be on your own.

I'm ok.

Call me when you arrive then.

Thumbs-up emoji

Bach limps in, from the room where there's a piano
and a telly and a glass sideboard full of tat.
I want to write but there's no room.
There is vomit on the underside of the chessboard.
I know your brother won't have said he's busy.
I try to call him but it's engaged.
It's raining out.
The beginnings of a storm (in April!).

I fold away the sunloungers.
Try to clear up, but all the cupboards are full
of shovelled snow from before.

We play dominoes.
My six-year-old son who said *I'll get you for this* has
invisible-inked fuck off across his tiny chest.
Scratchings of your agitated blood have stained the sheets.
The bed now spare again.

FROM HEARING THE NEWS

What I remember is how gentle your brother's voice was.

He sounded far out on a precipice.

I could hear he had no handrail,

but he was careful.

For me.

The generosity in that care,

was made of something delicate but strong.

THERE WAS NOWHERE ELSE TO PUT IT BUT STRAIGHT INSIDE MY CHEST

Water pours from me,
I pour.

The children are frightened by my inside-out sounds.

A neighbour comes round, puts them to bed, makes
strong tea with sugar, sits with me into the night, knee to
knee, on hard-backed dining chairs pulled awkwardly
to the centre of the room.

Nobody turns the light on.
We sit there in the dark,
unspeaking.

Until Mac gets home, leaves the door on the snib
so the neighbour can slip out.
Holds me still in one of those ox hugs of constraint.
All his weight against my chest,
to keep my heart in its tin.

ONLOOKERS / LOOKING BACK (FROM THE PLATFORM TO THE BEACH)

Was it a baptism or a rehearsal?

You reported 'finding grace'.

Spatter. Dispersal. Dissolution.

Witnesses

    (Did you steel yourself? Cry out?)

        walked home with you on their shoes.

ON PICKING OVER ALL
THE MESSAGES

Looking for evidence
in amongst the bare bones,
it's a scant meal to overpick.
Mealymouth of a script.

Before:

I'm ok. Winter blues I guess …

  u frgt Flo's jar. …

Just thinking out loud here – …

  Thanks for the lightbulbs u sent: much nicer

  (smile emoji …)

Not sure that's a good idea: ur holiday. …

  I'm kindof a state. What about Mac and yr kids? …

Dunno. I have lent on you too much. …

and after:

> Sorry – I am isck – prob me. …
>
> > Scrd. …
>
> I wish I'd styd for the storm with you. …

(Meanwhile, we left the kids in the car and stood on the
front, arms out, leaning on the wind. Without you.)

I see how I wrote myself in, inwritten,
slipped as a note unasked for,
under your door.

RETURN?

I picture you in the tunnel
On the tracks
A conclusion begun in youth
Now draws you back.

A return
To a tiny scratch
The concrete ache
That mark we made

12.11.1998.

A return
To the first page
The groove remains
The rails unchanged
And in between
The book you wrote
But forgot about the ink.

Blank   Between   Book Ends.

Into the cleave
The duct
The *and then* –
All the light we sucked.

I know this is *my* picture –
Glasgow was just happenstance.
That tiny dot of jouissance
Never really featured.

I know I am looking for hooks
Pegs on which to hang meaning.
Hashing out some plotlines
All of them with me in.

PISS

I am standing in the corridor of your brother's flat.

It is small.

There are five doors.

One I have just come out of.

One is open and leads to the kitchen.

The other three are closed.

Which is the bathroom?

I can't remember.

I am trying to remember.

But I can't.

I am trying to be as quiet as I can be.

They are all suffering with lack of sleep.

Their daughter is young and has been refusing bed.

Much has been made of the need for rest.

I barely know your brother.

Have never met his wife before.

I am unsure if I should be there at all.

At this most desperate of times.

Which is the bathroom door?

I can't remember.

My bladder is very full.

I am frozen here, in my nightie.

Crossing my legs.

I limp to the front porch.

I'll go in the garden.

I can't find a latch that would stop it from locking shut.

I imagine it clicking behind me and having to knock,

half naked, on the door.

Having to wake them, ask to be let back in

I try the kitchen windows.

Locked.

My bladder is very, very full.

I think about climbing into the kitchen sink.

Spot a large yoghurt pot, for compostable waste, on the side.

Empty it.

Take it to my room.

Squat.

Stop.

    (clench)

Worry about the noise of the piss hitting the plastic.

The flat is small.

I fold my pants into the bottom of the pot to sop and deaden the sound.

Squat.

Fill the pot to the top.

Carry to the kitchen.

Hoping not to slop.

Pour.

Wash.

Replace compost.

Wash knickers with Fairy.

Hang on radiator.

Sleep.

No one will ever know.

Until your funeral, when I will tell the story as a way of releasing tension as we pass around photos of you as a child in nappies.

PLANTING TOMATOES WITH YOUR BROTHER

On the steps outside your brother's place.
It's a domestic chore but we make a ritual of it.
Deliberately investing in a future,
where the past has been snapped off.
A process.

In morning light, we talk about your

>   Ob / abjection
>   Your love for the Underdog
>   ~~Sacrifice~~ Bravery? Statement?
>   Activism
>   Choice

Your niece is skipping in the street next to us.
I am bowled over by his patience with her.

That careful care.

She very quickly sucked my toe earlier, like a bite with-
out teeth, pretending to be a monster under the blanket.

It jangled me as we have barely met –
implicit trust – I wonder how salty it tasted,
and cold in her tender mouth.

As we hand each other the gentle plants, well out holes,
pat them full, their steamy tomato plant smell smoothing
us, I remember it warmly, as the sun blushed our
shoulders.

The nonviolentcommunication.

But I also remember the feeling of the moist grit in
my hands. The naked little roots with their tiny white
millipede legs, dancing in the air like raw nerves.
And that I just wanted to squat down.

Tug down.

And fuck that black and sweating soil tbh.

WITH YOUR BROTHER SORTING THROUGH THE FLAT

Holographic desire.
Mirror with nothing in it.
I want to bypass the edges of bodies.
Through timeframes
Through possibilities (although I know it's all impossible).
I wish I knew how to touch ~~him~~ you
without breaking everything and me in it.

I have so much to do and say
before the body starts to shutter up.
I know I am only high noon like this for a limited time.

I picture you two: bird brother brides, holding hands,
singing and ambling into the band of gold
where the sun draws a line across the disappearing sky.

We touch your stuff with care.
Make little piles.

Invest things with sentiment and significance
where there was none before.
Sort the tat from the sacraments.
Choose which are the symbols, props, backdrops.
Where to hang the scenes.

My pile is small:

> Potted plum
> A postcard from your fridge
> One of your coats (white-yellow-gold)
> A green-coloured jar from the shelf
> An empty frame
> A bike lock
> A kettle that shrieks

Anecdotes and condolences pour into your brother's
waiting lap like flowers. I put them in vases. And read on
repeat the memories from people who knew you before.

SIREN

You told me (and everybody else, it turns out) about
this toy police car you had as a child.
How you loved it until you noticed its lights –
there was something not right.
You couldn't love the car any more.
You were so angry with its wonky lights.
You smashed it against the fridge door.
You told me this to explain your rigid mind –
the inevitability of your terminal state.
Your future was crystallised in that siren light.
Finished to a tiny pile of eyeblue mind powder
and shat into the uncompromising sea.
I want to scoop you out.
Crush those blue lights and snort them.
I want to trash that police car and stick it in your big,
obvious, McFishy eye.
You fucking belligerent brainfuck.
Yes yes, fuck the police. But fuck you too.
Fuck you.

THE NAUSEA THAT SWEEPS ME AS I LEARN THAT I WAS NOT YOUR *ALL I'VE GOT*.

I learn that you kept your lifelines apart,
kept us all in the dark.
I learn about your brother's heart.

The space he made for you,
the key he cut for you,
the way he mopped your blood from his floors.

I learn that your illness was divisive,
how it played us, tricked us, snuck by us,
and eventually, scored.

WASTE

So here I am, bent over the dustpanning. Trying to learn
to heap all this spare feeling on the
People For Whom I Am Enough.

SAD IN PUBLIC

I'm not coming. Unless you want me to.
I don't want you to if you don't want to.
Well I don't want to. But I will if you want me to –
No, it's fine.   Why don't you want to?
I don't need to be sad in public.
k.   The kids want to come though.
Are you ok with that?
Yep.
You can manage?
It's fine.
Okay.
Love you.
Sure?
Yep.
About the kids I mean.
Yep.

YOUR ASHES

are not ashes at all.
They don't fly up
to join the wind and spirits
like they do in books.
They are heavy as shale or scree.
The grinding teeth of grief
pour heavy as sorrowbones
into the sea.

FROM TALKING TO YOUR COUSIN AT THE FUNERAL IN THE CITY

Laid out for the throng of mourners,
the kitchen feels like a theatre set.
I am not sure whether I am meant to be on stage too,
in the wings or in the stalls.
Or is this an interactive show?
I don't want to get it wrong and interrupt the monologue.
If that's what it is?
Her delivery is contralto.
She slips in and out of direct address.
Rhetoricals are left hanging between us,
like awkward guests unsure when to leave the room.
I don't know whether to step forward and help them out
(like wafting a moth away from the lightshade and
towards an open window) or leave them to dissolve
in their own time.

I feel compelled to validate this moment.

I can't think how to respond as audience, so I think I had better try and find my way into the script. But I am naked and she is fully clothed in nakedness and I feel this as an embarrassment. I am relieved when we are interrupted and I can cover myself in all the rags of accidental words again.

I realise I am uninterested in what other people have to say about *Why Things Are*. I resist hearing people shape and stamp your narrative. The more it is repeated and echoed around the room, the more fixed you become. In health you would resist this.
And so do I.

You don't belong in this scene – mundane possessions piled up. You are soaring somewhere elsewhere. The tangle of daily life that goes on is just a drag in the heat. Shit strewn from the door. It's like the house vomited.

Your brother and his wife are shut in a hunched-up room.
Your mum is reading the paper surrounded by boxes.
Your books are in the boxes.

Your bike shoes are in the bottom of the wardrobe,
smothered under a pile of pillows.

One of the twins was nearly sick in some tupperware,
the other drew a cloud on the skirting board.

Flo is making a game of it, at least.
The mould is alive, at least.
The ratstink from the basement
is teaming with microbes, at least.
I imagine all those glorious little maggots, eating
you back.

I have your lightbulbs in my pockets.

AND THEN IN YOUR KITCHEN
AFTER EVERYONE HAS LEFT

We revisit the monologue in snatches, boiled down now,
to the shortcutting short questions about responsibility,
culpability, guilt.

This time I am sitting on your kitchen counter swinging
my feet in my sister's shoes.

I'm looking down at my feet and thinking about how
I just took my sister's shoes without asking because she
is my sister and I know I can do that, and I am thinking
about *my* brother-my-tree, and the colour drains out of
me, out through my feet and my sister's brightly coloured
plimps – at just the mere glimpse of losing either of
them – and spills where the puddles of potion will be,
on the kitchen floor.

I am uninterested in the remaining WORDS in the room.

I am interested in the practices of enacting care, the rituals for making manifest unconditional love. The liberty to take each other for granted. The indulgence in that. I am looking at the colours swinging below me and the place where the potion will spill and I am thinking all this and I am thinking about your capability to upset – with the way you took for granted – and I am thinking of it as a way of enacting an indulgence in love unconditioned.

I am thinking about how the balance tipped. You became obsessed with the conditions you were in. You said the conditions were incompatible with life. You forgot about the unconditional bits and how you used to revel in and abuse them.

I am thinking all of this and hoping I am playing my part in the script in the room, so as not to appear rude, although to me it's already grey flakes of burnt, bleached printer paper falling onto the colourpuddle. The questions are extinguished as soon as they touch the air. Grey ash. It will all go in the pile for the skip at the front of the house.

I am already in the next morning, in your garden, urging
the potion that will be spilled, indulging the existence
of flowers and rocks and sweet-smelling cloves. I am
relishing ab/using all the ornaments and squandering all
the beautiful things on practical, everyday tasks. I will put
the fancy crockery in the dishwasher. I will glower on
holiday. I will eat you out of house and home and forget
to say goodbye. I will arrive without a plan and expect
you to come and collect me from an hour out of your way.
I will climb through any window I please. I will scuff and
stain these shoes and put them back in the cupboard
without mentioning anything.

And in return I hope you will do the same.
You can have anything and everything I possess and
have ever conceived of.
Why not.
Take what you like.
Unconditionally.

We will allow each other to take from each other without
acknowledgment. Those are the conditions.

Those are the fertile conditions for the potion the children will make and then pour on the floor and slip over in. Those are the unconditions we need for the magic we will cook and spill and then walk through with dirty shoes and bloody with the ash of pointless questions and daub on our wrists before leaving the front yard with the scaffolding in it and the emptied flat with your emptied-out mother in it and the street with the plum trees in it and the view through your landlord's lace curtains in it. The lace curtains I took down and folded and put in my bag and through which I will view all my own views now.

Which I will love, unconditionally.

UNDER THE CURTAIN

Somehow I can't leave your flat when everybody else does. I just abandon time and we passively outstay our welcome, until it's too late to get the tube.

Your brother has your room, so we four lie on your sofa bed, in the bay, under the curtain which has been taken down from the now-naked window.

> Mummy, when you're dead do you go mushy? / Does your tongue stick out? / Can children die? / Mummy what is 'or else'? / When you die can you still see? / Kit didn't look that sick. / Can I have a funeral? / Where's Kit? / Where's Daddy?

It feels as though we are lying outstretched in the middle of the road, my babies and me, in a pyjama nightmare. I draw them to me but it's not enough. The city light is glaring in and they are fitful. I flatten out some of the cardboard packing boxes and attempt to tape them to

the window. I sing a bit. I sing them words for everything
I can think of:

(and your bag...

and your cup...

and your Ninjago LEGO...)

until all I have left is a long list of body parts

(and your wrist...

and your eyebrow...

and your tonsil...

and your cuticle...)

which I name in tinier and tinier parts

(and your cornea...

and your pores...

and your imagined eyelash...

and your glottal stop...

and your undeveloped hormones...)

until every cell has a song and we are covered in the
petals of names.

By sunup the tape has come unstuck and the cardboard
shutters have left us bare and blinking.

GOING HOME

The plum tree is safe.

It is nearly in its new home.

It has attracted many admirers along the journey.

It has instigated many conversations.

It has kept me open and generous

Leaf canopy for the plum heart.

Up my sleeve: something of nature on the underground.

I shake fears about it not getting enough light.

I stroke its leaves.

Put aside worrying about the little holes in them

         Eaten through

I flick aside a terror of leaves shrivelling.

Fiercely protect it from clumsy strangers with heavy bags.

Carry it on my hip like a toddler.

Hold it high above the crowdhead going up the escalators.

I tell everyone who asks that you planted it
but you died and I am taking it home.
People can't believe the colour in it.
Neither can I tbh.

It does cross my mind that maybe it's not (impossible I
know because of all people you would notice when a
plum tree is) a plum tree and I talk myself through
how I will have to learn to love it anyway, even as a
copper beech.

I promise I will make jam from you.
And share it with whoever will listen.

WE MAKE OUR CONNECTION

On the way home I sit and wait for a replacement bus service in the station waiting room, opposite a man wearing brogues and (slightly grubby) construction trousers. He is reading a book about druids. He makes a comment about the circular architecture of the station waiting room – its conical roof – to some very non-commital women who just happen to be there, and I notice that he has a very posh voice. I ask him about the book. They were very cyclical, the druids, he says, and the women shift in their seats and raise eyebrows to one another, (no doubt my voice is posh too, pair of posh twats talking about circles) and I notice he has big, dry hands with round nails and I have a desperate urge to tell him that you killed yourself and that I have been at your funeral. So I do. And he is very kind in the way he listens. And when we cross the car park to the bus and the kids run to the back seats and I sit near the front with the tree up on my lap, he sits in the seat opposite me, across the aisle, and I appreciate that he didn't sit next to me. And we don't really talk more, but we both laugh when the bus driver's satnav gives him nonsensical directions and we both look out of our windows, from our different sides of the coach, kind of separately but together and I know that he, like me, has never really noticed this part of the countryside before, how green it is, even along the main road, and that we are noticing this together, from our different directions across the aisle. And just before I get off he offers me a sesame snap, which I very much want, and we shake hands, and as I am walking down the road from the train station and the bus is turning around in the car park so it can drive down the hill, I know that when the bus passes me he will give me a big wave from the window, and he does.

I enjoy the sesame seeds the second time around when I lie in bed picking them out of my back teeth.

RECOGNITION

We struggle to decide where to put it. In a forest by the
sea perhaps, in our garden at home, in that field at the back
of the holiday cottage, or on some random roundabout
somewhere in the middle of town, defying the traffic.
We decide on our village allotment. In fertile conditions.
Where the plums can be shared.

We have the tree soaking in a bucket of water. I dig the
hole while Mac helps the kids prepare their bits and bobs.
They wobble out in a line, their tokens porrect: a rook
and a knight made of modelling clay; a potato called
Captain Under Dog (bald no arms); a beanie you left at
ours years ago; an acrostic poem; a few mussel shells
unstuffed from a tracksuit pocket; a potion in an old
greenish jar.

We take turns to shovel the earth back in while the
other holds the slender trunk straight. The children
chatter, describe every thought and tread the loose soil

with their heels so that it fills their shoes and falls back down into the hole. With each thrust and bite of soil I earth another pulse:

There's the grief I felt for myself in motherhood
There's the grief I feel for my marriage
There's the grief I feel for you
There's the grief for my aging parents
For the child I was who wanted love unconditional
FOR ANY DOUBT I MAY HAVE EVER CAUSED
ANY OF YOU TO FEEL
For the adult I was who found I was right all along
For the I never new
For possibility
For trees
For too few photographs you can hold in your hands
For capability
For career
For academic passions
For revolution as event
For music I can't play
For all the flowers I have dug up and left in plastic bags and killed of neglect.
For the knowledge of the end of this mania.

After laying down their offerings the kids amble off to stick sticks in holes. Mac slides his back down a bigger tree. I sit beside him, lean in.

Silence.

bees buzz

Pour thoughts like careful water.

Hold you up to the light.

Take your weight.

Lay you gently in the moss.

I look into Mac's eyes.

I'm sorry.

He shrugs. Meets my gaze. Meets me there.

Preposterously honest.

You can never ask anyone to change a feeling.

We're all a bunch of cunts.

He kisses first me and then the tree, full on the mouth.

Eels slither into the river.

A whale unculls.

I know a thousand starlings will roost in your branches.

VOODOO

You gave me a book once, about voodoo. It explains the
magic of it, the process of possession.

Anyway I lost the book, in a devastating flood only
metaphorically related to this one, but this is it.
We do it.

To the tunes of your self-made music rack (synth words
like decay, sustain, release, attack), we oscillate the
forest, dance and stamp in the chaos:

All the spewk in the bin
All the stuff in discarded drafts
All the words on my list —
All the ones I used
All the ones I didn't
All the unborn beating hearts of beats

Into the air, we build towers of luminous blocks and we do not knock them down. We stretch and knead and beat ourselves a pulse, and out of that blurring, you push through us.

You are in us
You are in us

The movement of our bodies pushes at the limits of what's possible, butts against our windows, pushes at the way things are. You snake our necks and nod our heads, you make us pout.

You unfold us
You lift us as applause
The life force
Sun Ra breaks over the forest
Light shines on our faces
And a love supreme
Love in outer space
Radiates through the cosmos.

149

TEXT TO AN ABSENT FRIEND

It is 3.50 a.m. and I have just laid my head on the pillow. We drank our way through the entire fridge and chatted our tits off for hours after all the others were in bed. Danced our own private techno rave. So much love. So much grief – for Kit but also for the wasted times when we could have been together. We have spent all day in awe. Of Kit. Of us all. Your poem shook the whole forest. Everybody cried like fucking dolphins. I missed you so much. We swam in the sea. It was lush and cold and massive and Kit was in it. It was in us all. I love everyone. Do everything! Do it with love!

KIT

I owe you a book
The cover will be rough like brushed cotton but closer
Like an earlobe
The typeface will say your name softly
Each letter set with great care
It will sit lightly in the two palms' offering
Its pages will brush like moth legs
Or the hairs of the cochlea
The sound of the pages will be of spaces
Of soft Cs
Deliberate or fluttering
Depending on the speed of thought.
There will be spaces, clear blank spaces –
Space to think
And not think.
It will ask to be held with care
And it will receive with care
It will rest when placed
It will shimmer with edges of leaves and bark

And sunlight.
It will smell
Of your hair
And of time
And of whatever they put in ink that smells like it does
And of simple use of shadow.
It will be
What is, and nothing.
It will ask and be asked of, to be
Open
Unfolding
Willing
Willed
Encounter

Kit.

I owe you a book.
Will you write with me?
Shall we hold hands?
I know I am only high noon like this for a limited time.

We can jump together.

One two thr—

ACKNOWLEDGEMENTS

I can't find a source for the Dimitri Alexanych quote on the fridge magnet, but thank you. The loiter lines and the six-year-old son are with kind permission from Nicholas Johnson (*Cleave*, Waterloo Press, 2012.) 'Dog eat dog eat cat too' is from *Let There Be Rock*, AC/DC, 1977, Albert Productions.

I would like to thank the following people and organisations, without whom *Kit* would not exist: Arvon Foundation, Lisa Baker, Joe Barker, Phil Farr, Linda Fitzsimmons, Cynan Jones, Look UK, Max Porter, Steph Senec, Estelle van Warmelo, Writing Mill.

Thank you to everyone at Profile, Riot and Syndicut, Susan Wightman at Libanus Press, artist Andy Lovell and designer Sinem Erkas for the beautiful cover, Megan Sinfield for the title-page eel illustration, and all at the brilliant CHEERIO Publishing, especially my editor Martha Sprackland, for enabling this text to become a book.

I am also grateful for help and encouragement from my colleagues, friends and family, especially Aaron Berg, Sian Barker, Tom Bullough, Charlotte Carson, Shaunagh Craig, Rina Gill, Dave Kenicer, Charis Melvin, Peter Mimpriss, Alexi Murdoch, Sue Peebles, Richard Reed Parry, James Scudamore, Katie Sinfield, Nick Skinner, Angeline Tyler, Luke Williams, Jackie Wylie, Stuart Youens.

S, with love, thank you.

B, G, G, you tell the best jokes ever. I love you.